DATE DUE

GETTING INTO NATURE™

GETTING INTO NATURE™

Bees

INSIDE AND OUT

Text by Gillian Houghton
Illustrations by Studio Stalio

The Rosen Publishing Group's
PowerKids Press™
New York

Published in 2004 in North America
by The Rosen Publishing Group, Inc.
29 East 21st Street, New York, NY 10010

First Edition

Book Design:
Andrea Dué s.r.l., Florence, Italy

Illustrations:
Studio Stalio (Ivan Stalio, Alessandro Cantucci, Fabiano Fabbrucci)
Map by Alessandro Bartolozzi

Library of Congress Cataloging-in-Publication Data
Houghton, Gillian.
Bees inside and out / Gillian Houghton.
    p. cm. — (Getting into nature)
Summary: Describes the physical characteristics of honeybees,
where they are found, their behavior and social interactions,
and a brief history of beekeeping.
Includes bibliographical references and index.
ISBN 0-8239-4204-X (lib. bdg.)
1. Honeybee—Juvenile literature. [1. Honeybee. 2. Bees.]
I. Title. II. Series.
QL568.A6H58 2004
595.79'9—dc22

                                                    2003015523

Manufactured in Italy by Eurolitho S.p.A., Milan

Contents

The Bee's Body

The honeybee is an **insect.** Its body is covered with thick, waxy hairs and is divided into three parts: the head, thorax, and abdomen.

The head has two sets of eyes and two long **antennae**. Near the underside of the bee's head are the mandibles, or chewing mouthparts. Close by is the proboscis, which works like both a tongue and a straw. The thorax is the middle part of the honeybee's body, where its wings and legs are found. The rear part of the bee is the abdomen, which contains its major **organs**. At the very end of the abdomen lies the hidden stinger, which the honeybee uses to attack its enemies.

4

A honeybee
(*Apis mellifera*)

A Look Inside

The bee's brain sits inside its head. The thorax forms the center of the bee's body. The abdomen contains the bee's crop, a pouch where **nectar** is stored. It also holds the bee's heart, **glands** for making wax, and the organs that break down food. In the abdomen are also found the stinger, **venom** gland, and **reproductive** organs.

The bee depends on its senses to find food, defend its **colony**, make babies, and raise its young. Like humans, the bee has senses of sight, smell, taste, touch, and hearing. The bee gathers information very differently than we do, however. It uses its antennae, proboscis,

aorta

brain

thorax

antenna

pharynx

mandible

nerve ganglia

foreleg

proboscis

6

and feet, not its mouthparts, to taste food. Hairs on its antennae also sense smells. The bee "hears" through vibrations, or movements, in its legs.

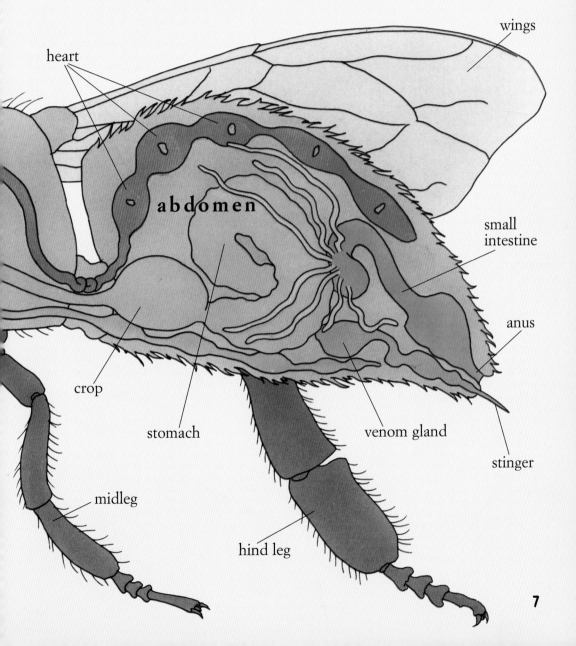

wings

heart

abdomen

small intestine

anus

crop

stomach

venom gland

stinger

midleg

hind leg

Bees Around the World

The earliest relatives of the modern honeybee first appeared on Earth some 40 million years ago. This prehistoric kind of bee, known as *Electrapis*, underwent many changes throughout the years. About 35 million years ago, the result of all these changes was a new type of bee, called *Apis*. *Apis* has not changed very much since then. The modern honeybee looks a lot like the prehistoric *Apis* and shares the same **classification** name. Scientists believe that the ancient *Apis* behaved much like the modern honeybee, **pollinating** flowers, making honey, and living with other bees in colonies.

Modern honeybees are native to Europe, Africa, and much of Asia. Between the seventeenth and nineteenth centuries, European settlers brought honeybee colonies to North America, South America, and Australia. Honeybees did well in these new places. They adapted, or changed, to meet the challenges of new climates. Today the honeybee is an important member of many **ecosystems** around the world.

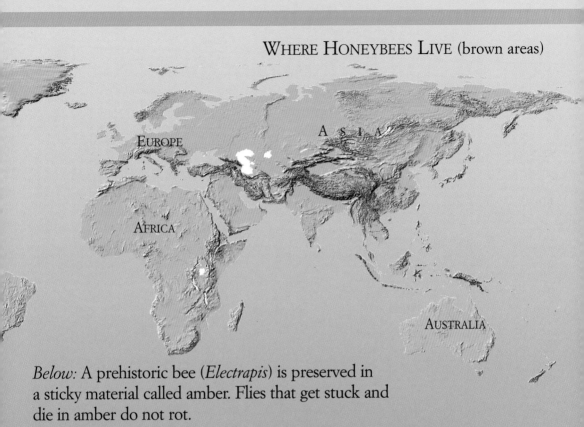

EUROPE

ASIA

AFRICA

AUSTRALIA

Below: A prehistoric bee (*Electrapis*) is preserved in a sticky material called amber. Flies that get stuck and die in amber do not rot.

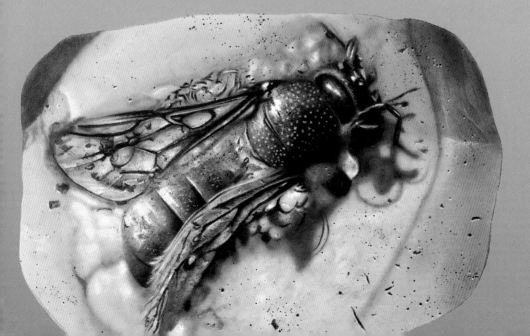

All in the Family

queen

drone

Honeybees live together in a colony. The members of a colony are divided into three groups: the queen, the drones, and the workers. The queen is the leader. She must mate with the drones of other colonies and lay eggs within her own hive. The several hundred drones of her own colony are her sons. Their only job is to **mate** with the queens of other colonies. The worker bees are the queen's many daughters. They can't lay eggs. As young adults, the 30,000 to 80,000 workers build the hive and defend it from enemies. They also take care of the honeycomb, where honey is stored.

Opposite, top: Three African honeybee pupae sit within their cells. Soon they will leave their cocoons as adult bees.

As adults, the workers take care of the whole colony by gathering food and feeding the queen and her several hundred drones. This is very tiring work. After only a few weeks of life, worker bees die.

worker bee

Below: This photograph shows the seven stages of bee growth from egg (*far left*) to pupa (*far right*). In the middle are larvae. It takes several weeks for an egg to grow into a larva, a pupa, and then an adult bee.

Welcome to the Hive

The hive is the center of a honeybee's life. It provides a warm home, a place to store food, and a nursery in which the colony's young can be raised. The hive is made from beeswax. Beeswax is a fatty combination of honey and pollen, which is produced by glands in the bodies of worker bees. It takes two pounds (1 kilogram) of honey to make enough wax to build a single hive.

The hive is a very well-made structure. It holds honeycombs that are made up of tens of thousands of cup-like holes, known as cells, which store honey. Each cell has six sides of equal length. The opening of each cell is angled up to prevent its honey from spilling out. The cell walls are paper-thin but are still able to hold many pounds of honey. Some 80,000 cells are joined together to form a two-sided sheet comb that hangs from the inside walls of the hive. A hive holds seven to ten of these honeycombs.

Below: This is a human-made hive known as a Langstroth hive. Within its box are removable wooden frames on which bees build their honeycombs.

Right: A bee hive in the wild. The hive's egg cells, containing eggs, larvae, and pupae, can be seen just above the cells where the hive's honey is stored. Worker bees tend both groups of cells.

Bottom, near right: A bee hive found in the hollow of a tree.

Bottom, far right: A human-made top-bar hive in which bees form hanging honeycombs on removable bars or slats.

Nectar and Pollen

During the seasons when plants flower, honeybees in mild climates gather and store the food that will last them throughout the cold winter. Bees live on nectar and pollen. Nectar is a sweet liquid produced by flowers and provides the main element of honey. It is an excellent source of carbohydrates, which are simple sugars and starches. Pollen is a fine dust also produced by flowers. Like nectar, it is very healthy and helps bee larvae and the queen live and grow strong.

proboscis

stigma

style

petal

anther

filament

ovary

Nectar and pollen are gathered from blooming flowers by worker bees called foragers. To forage is to wander and search for food. A worker bee can carry a load of nectar that is heavier than its own body. About 75 foraging trips must be made to collect enough nectar to make 0.035 ounces (1 gram) of honey.

Left: A close-up of a bee's head and its proboscis. The proboscis acts like both a tongue and a straw.

Below: A bee draws nectar from a flower using its proboscis. Meanwhile, the flower's pollen begins sticking to the bee's legs. Pollen falling from the bee's legs will help other plants produce flowers.

Let's Dance!

The survival of a bee colony depends on communication. Communication is sharing thoughts or knowledge. Bees learn and communicate through their senses of hearing and touch. Information gathered from their antennae and legs helps honeybees recognize the scents of at least 700 types of flowers and their locations. They can then communicate this knowledge to each other through visual messages known as dances. By vibrating, or quickly moving, its wings, a bee can make a buzzing noise that sounds throughout the hive and announces a foraging trip for nectar and pollen. Many scientists think that a returning forager tells other bees where to find pollen and nectar by doing a "dance." By moving in

circles, wagging her abdomen, and buzzing her wings, she may be giving her fellow bees directions to a rich supply of food that she has found.

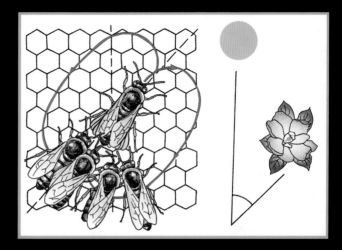

Above: This bee's waggle dance tells the workers that nectar and pollen can be found at an angle to the right of the sun.

Below: This waggle dance tells the workers that nectar and pollen can be found nearby, at an angle to the left of the sun.

Above left: A bee performs a round dance to tell other worker bees that nectar and pollen are within 35 yards (32 meters) of the hive.

Left: A bee performs a waggle dance to tell the workers that nectar and pollen are straight ahead, in line with the sun.

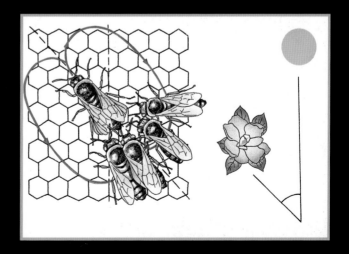

The Queen Bee

Each bee colony has a queen, a female bee who mothers the many thousands of members of the colony. A queen begins life like any other bee, as an egg. When the egg hatches, or breaks open, a **larva** comes out. A larva is a wingless, wormlike form that will grow into an adult bee. A queen bee larva is fed a sugary substance known as royal jelly. The other larvae in a colony are fed a less sugary food known as worker jelly. Both jellies are produced by glands in the mandibles, or mouthparts, of worker bees. Being fed royal jelly makes the queen bee able to mate and lay eggs. She will live as long as three years, while drones and workers live only a few weeks.

When a queen reaches adulthood, she has only two weeks to mate. She leaves the nest in search of male bees, known as drones. After mating, she returns to the nest. As spring approaches, she begins to lay her eggs.

Opposite, top: Fed with royal jelly, the queen will grow larger than other bees and be able to lay eggs. Her life is much longer than that of drones or workers.

Opposite, bottom: This is a photograph of a queen bee surrounded by dozens of her workers. It is their job to feed her and her drones, build and tend the hive, and guard the hive from enemies.

A Honeybee Grows Up

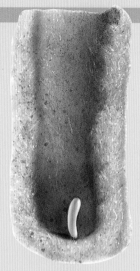

egg

Three days after they have been laid, the eggs hatch. Almost all of these larvae will grow to be worker bees. Worker bees are females who will never mate or lay eggs. Instead, they spend their lives serving the needs of the queen and the whole colony. The rest will become drones, the male bees that mate and reproduce but have no other job within the colony. After ten days, each larva spins a cocoon. The adult worker bees build a wax cap over the opening of each larva's cell. In this dry, warm space, the larva becomes a **pupa**. A pupa sits within a cocoon as its body begins to change from a wormlike form to that of an adult bee. After about three weeks, an adult bee leaves the cocoon. The queen will continue to lay eggs throughout the spring, constantly adding to the colony's population until there is no more room in the hive and no more food for new members.

Near right: An adult bee climbs out of its cell after its cocoon has fallen away.

Far right: These cells of an empty honeycomb hold bees in different stages of development from egg (*top*) to cocooned larva (*middle*) to adult bee (*bottom*).

larva   cocooned larva   pupa   adult bee

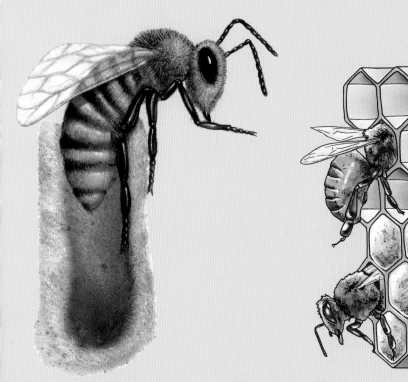

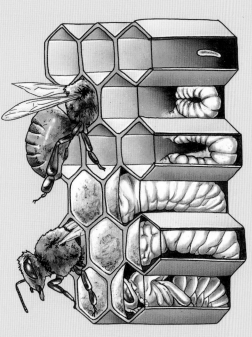

Honeybee Pioneers

By midspring, the honeybee colony may grow too large for its comb. In this case, the queen and about half of the colony's worker bees prepare to leave the nest in search of a new home. The queen lays several eggs, which are fed royal jelly. Just before the new queens emerge from their cocoons, the parent queen and her followers, known as the swarm, leave the nest. They gather on a nearby tree branch. Scouts are sent out to look for a new home. It must be well hidden, dry, and protected from the wind. It must have a small, easily guarded entrance, and it must be surrounded by flowering plants. When the scouts agree on a location, the swarm follows. Before winter, this new colony must build new combs of wax and collect enough honey to survive.

Back at the old colony, a new queen emerges. She will kill any other newly hatched queens by stinging them. She then becomes the ruling queen, and the life of the hive continues for another year.

Above: In this illustration, a swarm of bees leaves its old, overcrowded honeycomb in a hollow tree trunk to search for a new place to build a colony.

Above: This photograph shows a swarm of bees gathering on a branch before heading out together in search of a new home.

A Brief History of Beekeeping

Humans have enjoyed the sweet taste of honey for centuries. Cave paintings dating back 15,000 years tell us that prehistoric peoples gathered honey from hives in the wild. The sweet honey was used to keep meat fresh, sweeten foods, and make drinks, such as mead, which is similar to beer. Beeswax was used to make candles. In Indonesia, wax was used in batik printing to create colorful patterns on cloth.

Some of the most popular things made with the help of honeybees are shown here, including honey, candles, furniture wax, and royal jelly, which is used in makeup.

The first-known beekeepers were the ancient Egyptians. They created holes in mounds of unbaked clay in which bees could build combs and honey could be collected by people. In northern Europe, in the first century AD, beekeepers used baskets, called skeps, to house their bee colonies. In 1853, the first movable frame hive was invented. In it, each comb grew on a separate wooden frame. A hive much like this is still used today.

Above: An eleventh century book illustration shows beekeepers collecting a swarm of bees in baskets.

Right: This 7,000-year-old rock painting shows someone gathering wild honey from the inside of a tree. Some people still collect honey in this way.

HONEY

Glossary

antennae (an-TEH-nay) The pair of thin, threadlike sense organs on the bee's head.

classification (kla-suh-fuh-KAY-shun) The placing of things into groups that help define and describe them.

colony (KAH-luh-nee) A group of creatures of the same species who live together in a specific territory.

ecosystems (EE-koh-sis-temz) Communities of plants and animals that are living within certain areas of land.

glands (GLANDZ) A group of cells or an organ that removes materials from the blood and changes them into something new for use somewhere else in the body. Bees have glands that produce wax for use in building honeycombs.

insect (IN-sekt) Animals like bugs and bees that usually have three segments to their bodies and three pairs of legs.

larva (LAHR-vuh) The wingless, wormlike creature that comes out of a bee egg.

mate (MAYT) To join together two bodies in order to make babies.

nectar (NEC-tur) A sweet liquid produced by flowers that provides the main element of honey.

organs (OR-gunz) A group of cells or a body part that has a specific job to perform in the body.

pollinating (PAH-lih-nayt-ing) The act of carrying pollen to a flower, allowing it to reproduce.

pupa (PYOO-pah) The middle stage of development for a bee. After entering the cocoon, the bee larva becomes a pupa. It will leave the cocoon as a bee.

reproductive (re-pruh-DUK-tiv) Relating to the making of babies.

venom (VEH-num) A poisonous material that is used to attack enemies through biting or stinging.

Index

Web Sites

Due to the changing nature of Internet links, PowerKids Press has developed an online list of Web sites related to the subject of this book. This site is updated regularly. Please use this link to access the list:

www.powerkidslinks.com/gin/bee

About the Author

Gillian Houghton is an editor and freelance writer
in New York City.

Photo Credits